CREATING HAPPINESS

How a Million-Dollar Raffle Changed My Life

James Anderson

DUSTY ROAD
PUBLISHING
Denver, CO

Creating Happiness: How a Million-Dollar Raffle Changed My Life

Published by Dusty Road Publishing
Denver, CO

Library of Congress Control Number: 2015959052

Anderson, James, Author
Creating Happiness: How a Million-Dollar Raffle Changed My life
James Anderson

ISBN: 978-0-692-58854-3

SELF-HELP / Personal Growth / Happiness

QUANTITY PURCHASES: Schools, companies, professional groups, clubs, and other organizations may qualify for special terms when ordering quantities of this title. For information, email peakpro@comcast.net.

DUSTY ROAD
PUBLISHING

Denver, CO

ACKNOWLEDGMENTS

I am very grateful to the numerous spiritual and personal development teachers (too many to mention) that have assisted me through personal meetings, seminars, books, videos, and audio programs. Their knowledge helped me transform my beliefs about myself and the world, enabling me to change my thoughts and habits to create a new version and vision of myself. My trust in their ideas and guidance, in tandem with my own intuition, helped direct me on the path to greater happiness.

I am especially grateful to my editor, Alexi Paulina, for her friendship, guidance, and support. Her skillful editing and suggestions from the inception of my book idea were essential in creating this book.

I also want to thank Judy Goodman for her vision and original concept for the book cover, and Soori McEachern for her beautiful graphic design creation of the cover.

~~~

INTRODUCTION

———

I know what you're thinking: *How could not winning a million-dollar raffle transform a person's life in a marvelous way?*

The knowledge I have to share may challenge your rational mind at first, but after reading my story and learning what I did to change my energy and vibration, you'll see the value in it. This book offers much more than just theory and ideas. It's a real-life account of having moved from a state of chronic dissatisfaction and resignation to a place of joy and fulfillment—*a change I created from the inside.*

Quantum physics has shown that the observer affects what is observed. In truth, the observer creates what is observed. The higher your vibration, the more choices you have and the easier it is to manifest those choices. This is theory, and you've probably heard it a hundred times. I took this theory and applied it, with focus and consistency—and it changed my life.

It can change your life too.

How do I know this works? *Because I did it!*

~ ~ ~

Happiness is not something ready-made.
It comes from your own actions.

~H. H. Dalai Lama XIV

———

*Choose your thoughts carefully ... you are
a masterpiece of your life.*

~Rhonda Byrne, "The Secret"

———

Chapter 1

THE MILLION-DOLLAR RAFFLE

———

When I first read in the local newspaper about a raffle to win $1 million in cash or a house valued at $1.2 million, I was very excited. I had been practicing the Law of Attraction with some success and was always looking for new ways and new things to manifest in my life.

After practicing several techniques I had learned a few months earlier, I was hired for great position at a company I wanted to work for, so I had evidence that such methods work.

Winning the raffle would have been a much bigger creation than anything I had consciously manifested already. Certainly, a great job is excellent (and so was getting a few dates on the weekends), but I wanted to stretch my wings and go for something much bigger. There's no denying that a million dollars would be an impressive manifestation, not to mention the benefits it would bring to my life and my bank account.

Many experts in the Law of Attraction say the universe doesn't care if it's a cup of coffee or $1 million you want to attract—it's not more difficult for the universe to deliver the $1 million. It really is our beliefs and the alignment of our beliefs that determines the speed at which things manifest in our lives.

Before hearing about the raffle, I was listening to an audio interview with personal-growth expert Marci Shimoff, who talked about her book, *Happy for No Reason*, which I bought. Shimoff says that being in a state of happiness puts you on a fast-track to transformation. I was ready for a personal transformation.

My Life Before the Raffle

Before I entered the raffle, I had a lower base level of happiness than I do now. My fear in life was the greatest obstacle to my happiness. I always thought I would become naturally happy when I had the next big project at work, was in an amazing relationship, or was making a lot of money. You guessed it: I kept looking to the outside for happiness and didn't realize I had to create happiness from within. My goal was to win $1 million, and happiness showed up instead!

Fear had been a big issue for me since elementary school. Later in life, after doing a lot of personal development work, I realized that most everything I had been fearful about had occurred. The experiences ranged from a struggling business that became a failing business, to a failed marriage, to an overall lack of abundance.

It wasn't that I didn't work hard or lacked a strong work ethic. Though I was industrious, I kept sabotaging everything I was working toward due to my low self-esteem and fear of success. I hadn't been conscious of it most of the time, but the underlying factor in all my decision-making was fear. It was programmed on auto-pilot—always there, always running. Whenever I spread my wings or made a change, the fear was right there, dogging my every step, and eventually would step all over me and my new goals and dreams. After doing a lot of personal development work, the strength of my fear had diminished, but it was still there. All I had to do was to dream a little, and that sleepy giant would wake up and rattle the sabers.

Some things in my life were working, but they were not consistent—like work, for instance. I had great professional positions that usually didn't last long. Similarly, in relationships, I might start dating a fantastic woman and then it would end. The common factor in all these situations was, of course, *myself*.

I knew I was a congenial person to be with and had a lot to offer professionally and personally, so either I was attracting the wrong situations or somehow I was sabotaging them. Since I accept responsibility for everything in my life, I had to look at what I was creating.

I had lofty goals and dreams for work, financial freedom, and a fantastic relationship with a woman. Some of these things were showing up, coming and going briefly. I realized I was making some progress, just not the level of progress I wanted and had imagined. Though I was happy sometimes, joy was not an underlying emotion for me. While I was growing up, the emotional level in my life was flat—generally there was not much emotion, and the stronger emotion tended to be fear rather than happiness.

I was operating more from my head than from my heart. While I wouldn't have described myself as "heartless", my predominant mode of operation was to allow my brain to control all my decisions and behaviors. It was as if I was *going through* the process of life, not *living* the process of life.

I knew about the importance of living in the present moment, yet I wasn't experiencing that on a consistent (or even near-consistent) basis. I did discover and express my passions (after much work in this area as well), but at a basic level, I wasn't really happy with myself or my life. I was busy struggling to be or to get somewhere rather than choosing each day to live in a state of my preference, which is happiness.

I had always envied people who consistently seemed happy, and I wondered how they got there. My typical demeanor was more serious, with an attitude of "I've got work to do and have to get to it." I was coming from a place of *doing* rather than *being*, and the *doing* was not very happy.

With work, school, and other commitments, it seemed there wasn't time for fun. I had to be responsible. With all this going on, there wasn't time for happiness. Sometimes I did take time for play (hiking, camping, running, and playing sports), although I often viewed these activities as serious stuff as well. To me, life was serious business.

Looking back, I see that I probably could've done better in everything had I been more lighthearted.

Another reason for not being happy was that I was disappointed with my life. I didn't feel I had lived up to my expectations in for work, career, investments, and relationships, and I felt regret for some of the things I had done or not done. Yet, even if these outer things had met my expectations and I appeared more successful, I'm not sure that I would have been happy. I was looking for happiness from the outside, not from within.

I knew I had to be in a state of happiness to win the raffle. I didn't know what this state looked or felt like, but I made a plan to do things that would change my energy and allow me to have fun with the process. From everything I read and heard and believed, I knew I had to be happy to attract the things I wanted. I may have been thinking about it backwards: What I wanted was the million dollars, and my transformation to happiness became the benefit.

I also knew that if I kept working, practicing, and being open, that change would eventually happen. I would get to where I wanted to be on this journey and path I had imagined. I had heard enough stories of people who had come from situations far more difficult than mine and became very successful. So, I knew the slate was wide open and all I had to be was in alignment with my conscious and subconscious mind to manifest my goals and dreams. It was as if my "emotional thermostat" was set at a low degree of happiness and seemed to be stuck there.

This, I am pleased to report, was about to change.

~ ~ ~

A*ll that we are is a result of what we have thought.*

~Buddha

Chapter 2

WHERE I STARTED

———

I grew up in Detroit, Michigan, the home of Motown records and the Big Three auto-makers (GM, Ford, and Chrysler). My life was more focused on music and cars than on any type of spiritual growth. My family was Catholic and I grew up going to Catholic schools, but I do not consider this a spiritual upbringing.

How did I go from a middle-class environment in the Midwest to living in Colorado, where my personal and spiritual growth became the core of my foundation? Moving to Colorado was the easy part. Although a long story in the details, I'll just say I took an extended vacation and never moved back to Detroit.

I had a stable upbringing that was safe and secure. My father retired from Ford Motor Company after thirty-five years. My Mom raised five kids and started working at about the time my youngest brother was born. I went to a Catholic school for twelve years—plenty of discipline there. My father, a great provider, also was big into discipline. I loved my parents but was afraid of my father. The combination of the fear instilled by the school's Catholic environment and my father left me with a deep fear of life.

My brothers, sister, and I never were really encouraged or discouraged from doing anything. If we wanted to get involved with an activity in or out of school, as long as it was considered acceptable and not dangerous or expensive (and we asked permission to be involved), that was fine with my parents.

My family life was very secure, stable, and mostly harmonious. Anger rarely was expressed except for when we did something my parents considered wrong. My dad got mad at my mom only once in my recollection. My parents were social with our relatives, and our family always took a summer vacation, traveling throughout Michigan and other parts the country.

Despite not having a negative or dramatic family life, deep down I wasn't all that happy. Yes, we laughed and enjoyed many good times together, but there were not passionate exchanges—things like getting really loose and silly, or singing or dancing around the house. Our home life was more toned down, at a flat energetic and emotional level.

My parents were certainly not cold, nor were they very warm, affectionate, or feeling-oriented. It was the way they had grown up, so I hold no blame or anger toward them. My parents did the best they could with what they knew and who they were, and for that I am grateful. I did feel loved, although it wasn't expressed openly as affection.

When I showed more emotion in school, or at times at home, the adults around me would say it had to be toned down. Nuns at school would yell, tell us to be quiet, and give us the "evil eye." When playing too loudly at home, my siblings and I were told to keep quiet, so I didn't really have an emotional outlet. I didn't realize it at the time, but my emotional expression was squashed. I felt expressionless, with a lack of emotional energy and passion. As I look back, honestly, my life experience was kind of boring.

I was always energetic physically; playing sports was an outlet for me then and still is today. What I learned later (and created for myself) were ways to express my feelings, emotions, passion, happiness, and joy.

These last few areas—emotion and passion and joy-came much later, after college, and it was not an easy process to unleash and express myself. The happiness and joy part came last. Although I was happy at times, the basic sense of being happy was not present. My happiness set-point was low. It's not that I didn't have any fun or laugh; it's just that happiness was not a stable component of my experience. What seemed to be my core component was fear and insecurity. I didn't realize how much fear was present in my subconscious until many years later, after I understood the laws of attraction and energy flow and had read the *Conversations with God* books by Neale Donald Walsch.

All my life I had a fear of authority dating back to Catholic schools, my father, and life in general. I attended Catholic schools from kindergarten through twelfth grade. Many years later, when I started my business, I realized that my upbringing had not been much of a help for achieving business success. In addition, my personality as a people-pleaser added to my challenges for growth and reaching a higher potential. I would do whatever I could to have people like me, behaving as a chameleon type of person. While flexibility is good in some situations, I felt I had lost my identity and self-confidence by taking this approach to life. When you spend your time doing what you think others want you to do, you never really know what you want or like.

I Was a "Doer"—Always Busy

Growing up, my siblings and I always had a list of things to do around the house for my dad: painting, cutting the grass, cleaning the yard—typical things you have to do when you're a kid. I'm sure my dad had his list as well, and our duties were part of that list. My life seemed like just one big list of things to do. Sure, there were fun things on the list as well, but they aren't the ones that come immediately to mind.

I ask myself now, was I my list, or was I just doing the things on my list? Is that who I was? That certainly is not true now, but it may have been years ago. Does this really describe me, the things I enjoy, or my life purpose? I was not very self-reflective at this time in my life because I was too busy doing things.

I also didn't understand the difference between

religion and spirituality. During my Catholic-school upbringing, I had never even heard of spirituality, although I had plenty of religion. In grade school we went to church every school day, five days a week, and on Sunday we attended church with our class. Then I joined the church choir, which required me to attend an 11:30 a.m. mass on Sunday for the choir in addition to the 8:00 a.m. service with my class, so I was going to church seven times a week. Maybe it wouldn't have been so bad if I had felt enriched by the experience rather than being told how bad I was ("a sinner") and hearing the same old story about hell and heaven.

In high school there was less church influence in that we went to mass only once a week, on Fridays. On Sunday we were on our own. After high school, I was done with going to church. After so many years of being forced to do something that provided no rewards emotionally or spiritually, I'd had enough. It wasn't until a few years after college that I thought about God or religion very much. I felt that I was by myself in this thing called *life*, that there was no one helping me—not family or friends, let alone God, whoever he was. While I was not a self-professed atheist, I didn't much care about God, nor did I think he cared about me or was there to help me.

I had started a business a few years after college and struggled with the business and personal relationships for several years. Then I met Terry Lynn, a woman like none I had met before, and eventually we married. She was involved with spirituality and studied Buddhism. I certainly had heard of the Buddha and Buddhism, but didn't know much about the teachings.

My Spiritual Journey

I had a difficult time distinguishing between religion and spirituality, which I had at first put into the same category. That's all I knew, and it just confused me even more. Terry Lynn would tell me to find my own spiritual path, which was some of the best advice I've ever received.

I was living in Denver, Colorado, at the time. In Boulder, just north of Denver, there are many spiritual groups and people to connect with, so I decided to search for a path and a way for me to understand spirituality. I investigated many groups, read the brochures, and went to meetings to understand what they were about. I did connect with these groups somewhat, but many seemed more into a business of spirituality than about a path of meaningful evolution. The message with some was that to gain higher levels of spiritual growth, you just needed to pay more money to the organization. I found that a rather interesting approach, to pay more money to become enlightened. It didn't sound right to me, so I continued with my search.

After researching seven to ten organizations, I came across one called the Art of Living. They had a local Boulder branch; the main group was founded and operated out of India. The guru was named Sri Sri Ravi Shankar (for short they called him Pundigit). I decided to learn more about this group and to get involved with it because these folks seemed more concerned about their participants' well-being and helping them live their lives in connection with a higher spirit. The organization wasn't all about money. Yes, they charged fees for their weekend course and five-day course, but the fees were minimal for the amount of time involved, and were substantially less than what other organizations charged.

They offered various programs; the first was a three-day introductory course that taught a breathing technique call Kriya Yoga. They also had a five-day silent retreat, as well as weekly *satsangs* where participants could do yoga, sit in quiet meditation, or listen to an audio-guided meditation by the guru. These guided meditations involved rhythmic breathing that symbolized the vibrations of the universe, helping participants enter a meditative state and then easily move into a deeper meditation.

One of the first things I was told by the facilitator of the Boulder group was to read the book *Autobiography of a Yogi* by Paramahansa Yogananda. The book opened a new world for me regarding human potential. It was like waking up to a new reality, and was a life changing experience. After learning what the great yogis of India were doing—the miracles they were performing as part of their everyday lives—my thoughts on our capabilities had almost no limits. There was a whole new world of possibilities! I wanted to learn, be, and do more with my life and my potential. I just had to get started!

In the first week of my meditation practice, I had an incredible experience. After the guided breathing and meditation, I lay down and felt electrical pulses moving up and down my spine—like electric jolts to my body. I was a little scared at first, wondering if I might catch on fire or go into convulsions, but mostly I was intrigued. I observed the pulses that ran up and down my spine until they finally settled down and stopped. I never experienced that again. This energy awakened me to a new state, and I knew it was powerful.

Another thing I was introduced to at the Art of Living (and I know this may seem unusual to some) was the concept of people hugging each other. I didn't know how to respond at first. I had hugged before, but only with close female friends. Members of my family were not huggers. Sure, I hugged my parents and grandparents when I was younger, but I didn't hug anyone else in my family that I can recall, at least not until many years later. So, I reluctantly gave people hugs at first.

Now I want to hug almost everyone I see and meet! I do have to be careful at times, especially in business situations or when the other person is not open to it at all, but I usually make the effort anyway. You never know— maybe they needed a hug that day.

I continued for a few years with retreats and weekly satsangs. Later I stopped going on a regular basis and continued the practice on my own at home (I still do it almost daily). Yet, I felt there still was more for me to do.

The Fear Factor

My life still had challenges— I felt that fear was controlling me and how I reacted to situations. While some things had improved, I had some underlying beliefs that still limited me. One day I realized that everything I was (or had been) afraid of came true.

The struggling business that failed, the marriage that ended—the things I was most afraid of actually came to pass. This was serious! I struggled with my work and my marriage, and ended up declaring personal bankruptcy because of my problems with the business. My marriage ended in divorce. I found new, good work but for some reason it was inconsistent and didn't last long. I had an underlying fear that I wouldn't be successful or be happy.

A Change Was Coming

While reading books and studying ways to lose my fear and insecurity, I came upon a company that provided outdoor trips the included activities such as hiking and river rafting. HeroQuest learning adventures were aimed to foster personal, professional, and spiritual growth. I thought this would be good for me because I loved outdoor adventures and felt it would help me on my spiritual path. I called the owner, Josh Cohen, to find out more about these trips. One in particular seemed to work best for me: a seven day canoe trip on the Colorado River. We would put our canoes in the water just below the Hoover Dam. I was excited and couldn't wait to go, but it would take me year a year to get there. Some of the trips were scheduled only once a year. I had missed the first trip in the fall and would have to wait another twelve months to sign up for the next one.

I planned and anticipated this trip for the next twelve months, but almost did not get to go. A blizzard hit Denver the day I was planning to fly to the meeting area outside of Las Vegas, Nevada. I was devastated! The roads to the airport—and then the airport itself—were closed. I stayed in contact with Josh and things worked out. The next day the weather cleared and I flew out, arriving a day late. The boats had already left but were not too far down river. Two people paddled upstream to pick me up the next morning. I was waiting on the shore and shed tears of joy when I saw the boats coming. I knew this was going to be a powerful trip.

About a week before the trip, Josh had recommended that I get a copy of *Conversations With God (Book 1)* by Neale Donald Walsch. He said we would talk about it during the trip. Little did I know how powerful this book was about to become in my life! As I started to read it, many understandings came to me about my life—how things worked and how things didn't work. I read about the author's background in a Catholic school that sounded similar to my experiences. His understandings and misunderstandings of how life was working or not working for him paralleled my thinking. I cried while reading the book because I too didn't understand how life was supposed to work with God and the universe's role in our lives.

As Neale would say, *why doesn't anyone ever tell us this information?* Since then I have read Neale's first five books and reread *Book 1* numerous times. Like Neale, I felt I had been misled by the Catholic Church. I had been angry at the Church for awhile, and now was even angrier because I could see that it was mostly about control rather than spiritual freedom. I wanted the freedom! This book and others put me on a fast track to realizing that the universe will—and does—work for us every time if we let it and get out of our own way.

I had a great week on the Colorado River on the border of Nevada and New Mexico. During the trip we went through several exercises to gain insight into our life purpose. Yet, it was what happened when I returned from the canoe trip that started me down a path of a more expansive and determined spiritual and personal growth that continues to this day.

After the trip, I went back to the "real world," figuring out how to incorporate my experiences and lessons from *Conversations with God* into my daily life. My life had been built on fear, and the fear still continued as an unconscious belief. I was always sitting on the fence, afraid to completely jump over, scared to fully commit to my goals and dreams. Fear would come in and stop me from moving forward. This was frustrating on so many levels because I could never fully commit. I was very disappointed in myself and felt trapped.

In *Conversations With God (Book 1)*, one of the messages to Neale was to watch his thoughts and see where they went on a daily basis. This is not an easy task, but I was determined to change, so I did this every day for the next six months. I was running my own business at the time, and this practice was not very good from a business standpoint. In fact, it was one of the worst times for me financially because I was so unproductive in my work. I would spend a lot of time each day watching my thoughts and noticing what was I thinking or how was I thinking.

I would see my fears come in, recognize them, and work to gently move away from the fear. The fears would continue to come back over and over as strong, relentless thoughts. What I've learned about the unconscious mind is that we are programmed at an early age with thoughts, feelings, and emotions, and it can take a lot of work to change and make corrections in this belief system.

Things did get better over time. I could recognize the fear and tell myself that it had no power over me and would disappear. I felt better and was becoming more productive, but I lost a lot of time and money in the process and my business was suffering. I was borrowing money to keep it going. Finally I had to stop and declare bankruptcy and then started rebuilding my work and my life.

My fear was like a ball and chain that kept me from going very far and would pull me back when I tried to move forward in a significant way. I felt as if I were on a leash that stretched enough to make it seem that I was making a little progress before I got pulled back to where I'd started. What made it even harder was that I knew I had great potential but couldn't seem to get out of my own way. My self-doubt and insecurity seemed to be getting worse. My marriage also ended during this time, and I was feeling almost like a complete failure.

Keeping Active

It was the athletic part of me that kept me going during this time. I was a runner and continued to run 5K and 10K races and to keep in good shape. My athleticism was saving me from a complete breakdown. Outside of running, I was feeling pretty miserable.

One thing I always seemed to possess was determination and persistence, even if at times it seemed I was moving in the wrong direction. I would not accept defeat! Whenever I had a challenge in life, I rarely backed away. Challenges just made me dig in and push harder, because I was determined not to be a loser. At times I would get a bit lazy about things, but did what I needed to do to address a challenge.

When the pressure was there, I generally rose to the occasion. From weightlifting in high school I had developed strength and determination that enabled me to outshine others, and I was working to get my running times as fast as I could for a race. This determination also extended to professional areas such as public speaking.

Personal Growth

In 2007 I was introduced to a personal development

and leadership program with an organization called PSI seminars. During one of the exercises in a men's leadership program, we answered a series of questions. Based on the results, we were divided into groups. My group had many good qualities. Interestingly, one of our shared characteristics was that we were determined not to lose. (To be clear, *determined not to lose* does not mean *determined to win!*)

This realization hit me right between the eyes, so to speak: I didn't see myself as a person out to win; I was determined not to lose. All those years I had been working so I would not lose, not necessarily to win. *Winning* and *choosing not to lose* may sound similar, but there is a huge difference. It seemed that all my life I had been choosing not to lose.

~~~

When you change your inner world,
your outer world also changes.

———

Chapter 3

How I Started Living Once I Decided I Was a Winner

———

You must imagine that you are already experiencing what you desire. That is you must assume the feeling of the fulfillment of your desire until you are possessed by it and this feeling crowds all other ideas out of your consciousness.

~Neville Goddard

Entering a raffle to win a $1.2 million home or $1 million in cash, I knew my life certainly would change if I won, but I had no idea that *not* winning the raffle would also change my life—and a change it in a way that came as a complete surprise.

How could a raffle change my life when I didn't win? One might think I'm crazy to assert this, or perhaps that I'm just lying. One might even think that after not winning I would be depressed, but that was not the case at all. I became totally happy even after I didn't win. In this book you will learn how I accomplished this—and how you can do the same.

Once I started living from a happier place, my life seemed so much easier. Life no longer felt like a struggle, and people were more interesting to me. I also found people were more interested to meet and know me. My daily life and the quality of my relationships improved. I woke up each day from a happier place, with a smile on my face, ready to go out and make the best of my day. I wasn't so attached to outcomes. I still had expectations but lived more in the moment. And that moment was a happy moment.

Earlier in my life I was a people pleaser; now I was less concerned about what people thought about me. If I knew someone that acted negatively toward me or had a problem with me, for whatever reason, it did not bother me. I knew it was their problem, not mine. I would still be friendly to them, say hello, and have fun with whatever response I received.

I could not *think* my way into happiness—I had to take action, to change my energy and vibration.

To put myself in a state of happiness I used information, tools, and techniques related to the Law of Attraction—things I had learned over several years. But a greater change took place from the time I entered the raffle until the day of the raffle drawing. Later in this book I will reveal all the ways I have learned to intentionally and effectively use the laws of attraction.

Things Started Happening

It was time for me to get not just a tune-up, but a whole new engine—a different engine, one with more horsepower. In computer technology-speak, I needed a new operating system, not just a new version of the same system.

I had learned about many tools and techniques and applied them on some levels, but to make a bigger change I had to get out of my comfort zone. One way of doing this was to act as if I already had won the raffle. This may sound challenging, and it was. How you do act as if you are a person you've never been before? I had to ask myself what it would look like, feel like, and sound like to be a wealthy person. I observed successful, wealthy people and asked myself, *how would they act? What do I see in them, and what might others see in them?*

I realized I didn't have to change my personality; I just had to make it stronger. I asked myself, *what impression do I want to make with people, including myself?*

I became more extroverted and would start talking to people wherever I went. The conversations usually weren't very long, but I would be friendly and have fun talking to all kinds of people. I was also laughing more—laughing at myself and laughing with others.

Throughout my life I already had become less introverted, but now I was on a new level and felt very comfortable being more social. It felt natural, not forced. I realized that being happy and friendly is our natural state; we are just trained and conditioned not to be so.

In addition, I started feeling more successful, confident, and sure of myself. I no longer questioned things I did or said, wondering what others might have thought about them. My life seemed to go more smoothly, and my dating experiences improved. It was easier to talk to a new woman, and after a brief conversation I would ask if she wanted to meet again. I was less concerned with rejection, and most of the time was not rejected.

I felt I had more to offer, and my communication skills improved because I wasn't questioning everything I was saying or thinking. Words and communication just flowed, and I was finding that it was other people who seemed more timid and shy. I was just having fun. I felt like I was more interesting than I had been previously. It wasn't that I had so much more new knowledge; it just all came out, like the doors to my expansiveness had opened and I emerged. I enjoyed sharing myself and my interests and passions.

Although I was feeling a change during this time, I wasn't thinking about it much until after the raffle was over and I knew I hadn't won. At this point, you might say I was just doing individual assignments (which you'll read about later in the book) that put me in a happier state. I did not yet see how the different pieces of the puzzle were starting to fit together.

To use a basketball analogy, I was practicing the various basic skills such as dribbling, layups, running, and free throws—all separately, but when they were put together, I was playing a new game and having fun.

I had more energy as well. I would wake up earlier with high energy and would still have energy well into the evening. I also started getting more active athletically and began training for a triathlon, which was something I had thought about for several years. I committed to doing one triathlon, and then ended up competing in two more in the next few months. I was seeing life through a different set of eyes—everything seemed richer and more interesting and colorful, and I felt the curiosity of a child. I remember visiting New York City on a business trip and going to the Metropolitan Museum of Art, feeling fascinated with everything. I could have spent days there without becoming bored or tired. Overall, I had a greater awareness and appreciation of my life and everything in it. A quote by Wayne Dyer sums this up perfectly: "Change the way you look at things, and the things you look at change."

Who would have thought that living in a state of happiness could change so many things about my world? Many personal-development experts say that when you change your inner world, your outer world also changes. How true I learned this was!

~~~

*Anytime you expand yourself and your ideas
about who you really are and what you can really do,
your whole life changes.*

———————

Chapter 4

An Unexpected Outcome

———

Overcoming attachment does not mean becoming cold and indifferent. On the contrary, it means learning to have relaxed control over our mind through understanding the real cause of happiness and fulfillment, and this enables us to enjoy life more and suffer less.

~Kathleen McDonald

What a surprise it was—learning that I didn't win the raffle, yet discovering I was a different person anyway.

As you might imagine, I was getting pretty excited as the drawing date approached. I kept up my daily program of visualizing and all the other activities I'd been engaged in to manifest winning the raffle. I practiced what I had learned: that it was important to continue the actions to move toward one's dreams and goals without becoming attached to the results.

I was using all my senses to see, feel, and touch the million dollars and to be in the new house. I would smell and taste the food I was cooking in my new home and feel myself enjoying the time with friends and family, relaxing in the main living area and all the other areas around the home. I was fully engaged—I felt great and felt that I was already the winner, at least in my mind and energy.

An Unexpected Problem

An interesting thing happened a week before the drawing date. I had been working at a company as a contractor. The plan was that after three months I would move into a full-time position. Exactly a week before the drawing date, I received a call from my supervisor. (He was based in New York and I was located in Denver.) He said that my position would not become a full-time position and that my contract would last only an additional three months.

This news was a shock, and it threw my energy completely off—to the point that I almost went into a tailspin. Although my contract would not end for three months, I descended into a fearful state of mind. I lost my focus and passion for the contest and became more concerned about my work. Though I still did my daily practice to manifest winning the raffle, it wasn't the same. I was struggling to maintain my upbeat, positive energy and doing what I could to keep the fear from escalating out of control.

After several days, I calmed my fearful state and put all my energy into the raffle. Feeling that I lost valuable time, I wondered if the loss would be a problem for me.

By the end of the week, I was feeling strong again. Just a day before the drawing, I felt I was back to where I had been vibrationally or energetically before I had heard the news about my work.

The Day of the Raffle Drawing

The day arrived—an exciting day for me. After all my work, effort, and practice, I was about to learn if I had the proper energy vibration or alignment to bring the winning of the raffle into my reality.

Let me emphasize that for me, this endeavor was

major. It was not just a cup of coffee or an evening date that I was creating and manifesting! To the universe, of course, winning the raffle was not a big deal, but for us earthlings, such things are a big deal. To manifest them, we have to be in complete alignment with our request. This raffle would tell me if I truly understood and was in alignment with my desire by using the Law of Attraction—if I had applied my techniques and energy correctly. If so, the universe would shower me with the fruits of this wondrous example of my manifestation powers.

Since the raffle was held on a weekday, I was working that day and went about my normal routine of meetings and calls. I had to wait until the results were posted on the website the next day. My belief was that, until the results were actually posted on the website, the raffle was still mine to win.

I had *owned* winning this raffle in my own reality, and I was sincerely hoping my reality was the same as the one the universe had in mind.

I went to bed that night continuing with my visualizations and feeling that I was the winner of the raffle.

The Raffle Winner Announcement

When I rose the next morning, the first thing I did was check the website to see the names of the winners. There were several winners, actually. The grand prize or first-place winners were for the $1.2 million home and $1 million in cash, and there were several other winners listed that had won sizeable cash prizes.

As quickly as I could, I read through all the prizes and the names associated with each prize. Alas, my name was nowhere to be found! I wondered what I had done wrong, and what had been in the way of my winning. Did I have a limiting belief regarding abundance for myself, or was my vibration just not high enough? *What could have I done differently or better?* I wondered.

Several such thoughts went through my mind. Since the raffle had been for a well-established and reputable nonprofit organization (the Boys and Girls Clubs of America), I knew it was legitimate.

After thinking about this for a few days, I just let it go. I knew I had a good life and I was still having fun, so I really had nothing to complain about.

Days went by, and I was busy with work and my life. I stopped my manifesting routine regarding the raffle, although I still practiced daily with other desired manifestations in other areas. I withdrew my energy from the raffle and focused it elsewhere.

Something Was Different

A few weeks later, I realized I'd been in a very happy mood for days without intentionally doing anything to create it. Then I recognized that something was different about me—clearly, I had changed! My entire being of energy had shifted to a high state of happiness. Nothing seemed to bother or worry me. I wasn't feeling fearful about my work; I was just in a happy, peaceful state of being.

Since I often read books and listened to audio programs about the Law of Attraction, I continued this practice because I enjoyed it. Such activities always elevate my mood and energy, so there was no reason to change this habit, which was a big part of my life.

By entering the raffle and practicing all the things I did, I moved out of my old comfort zone and into a new world—a happier world that now was my new paradigm. It was at a new, higher threshold. I realized that this benefit was at least as important as winning the raffle would have been, although of course it would have been wonderful to win a million dollars in cash.

I now had a gift that would last me a lifetime, and beyond! I had opened a new door—engaged a new frontier and expanded into new world. People, places, and experiences emanate from this state of being. And it's a much more enjoyable state than my previous states of fear, lack, and worry.

You see, I really did win, and I won a much bigger game than I had realized I was playing! Anytime you expand yourself and your ideas about who you really are and what you can really do, your whole world changes.

There still is much more for me to do and to change; I'll never stop growing. This was just another step on my path to reaching my highest potential. Yes, it was a big step, but not nearly my last. I want to experience even more in life, and now I know I have the courage and ability to go the next steps and beyond.

~~~

*We all have the power to consciously shift
our vibration anytime and anywhere.*

Chapter 5

WHAT EXACTLY DID I DO TO GET HAPPY? (THE PROCESS AND STEPS)

———

Your life is the sum result of all the choices you make, both consciously and unconsciously. If you can control the process of choosing, you can take control of all aspects of your life. You can find the freedom that comes from being in charge of yourself.

~Robert F. Bennett

In this chapter, I'll share with you the process I used—the steps I took to move into a state of happiness when I was feeling less than joyful. None of these practices is mandatory; I suggest you try them all and use the ones that most appeal to you.

Find Music That Makes You Happy

Why is music so life-changing, and what does it have to do with our everyday life?

As modern scientists have discovered (and ancient mystics already knew), all physical matter is in a state of vibration. Everything that exists in our emotional, physical, mental, and spiritual world is based on vibration. And, as it turns out, a meaningful and happy life is the outcome of tuning oneself to a higher level of vibration (also known as *spiritual consciousness* or *divine consciousness*). The goal is to make a conscious choice to live every day from this higher level.

No doubt you have noticed how different music affects your mood. When listening to music, you are absorbing the vibration of sound, and it is affecting every cell in your body. Yes, that's right: Trillions of cells are being affected, and this vibration actually changes matter. Music is *organized vibration*.

Your brainwaves, breath, and heartbeat will sync with the vibration of music. That's why different types of music can put you in different moods. The sound vibration is sending messages to your brain and throughout your body, affecting brainwave patterns, hormone levels, heart rate, and your state of consciousness. Your body is responding—all its cells, organs, and tissues are vibrating and interacting with each other and with the outside environment. Just as outside vibration influences us, our internal vibration affects the outside world, as well as affecting our health and well-being.

It's easy to be influenced by others' energetic vibrations. Most of us were not raised to take charge of our vibration. The good news is that we can shift this energy vibration easily and consciously. We all have the power to consciously shift our vibration anytime and anywhere.

Without a steady, consistent state of vibration, our energies and moods can change frequently throughout the day. That's why it is important to stay consistent on the frequency you desire. If we don't set a consistent vibration, we can be influenced by other people or external energy vibrations in ways we don't prefer. By staying true to our higher vibration, we are less affected by external forces. We can choose moment to moment how we want to feel and interact with the world.

Prior to entering that raffle, I knew I wanted a higher vibration.

Sing and Dance

You can change your energy in seconds—for instance, by listening to upbeat music. I have quickly changed my energy on many occasions by listening to music I enjoy. I also like to dance, and when I go to a place where music is playing, my mood changes instantly.

While driving in Denver one day, I was wondering what would be a good song to get my energy pumping, change my attitude, and lift my spirits. What would be a good song to start my day on a high energy vibration?

Almost right after I had this thought, a fun song came on the radio: *Love Shack* by the B-52s. I've always liked the song; it makes me feel happy and playful. After hearing it on the radio that day, I bought the CD so I could listen to it whenever I wanted to.

After waking up each morning, I would have some coffee or tea and take a shower. When I was feeling fairly awake, I would play *Love Shack* to energize myself. Of course there are many songs from many artists that may have this effect on various individuals, but this one worked well for me at the time. I would play the song and sing along and dance around the house like I was onstage performing. Now, remember that I said I had to get out of my comfort zone, and so do you!

So, no matter how strange this suggestion may seem to you, just do it. It gets easier each time and will raise your mood and energy almost instantly. This practice moves your energy vibration to a higher frequency, and the universe responds more quickly to a higher vibration because you become more in alignment with the universal energy. After days and weeks of dancing around the house, it will seem as natural as brushing your teeth. After doing this, my energy would explode into a happy state.

I like to dance, so this was not difficult for me, but remember that it was seven in the morning! Many times I didn't feel like dancing, but I did anyway. I knew I had to be persistent and consistent to maintain this higher vibration. Once a week would not be enough—this had to be a daily practice and was best done in the morning.

When making changes or shifts in your life, remember that they do not always come easily at first. If they did, you might have been doing them already! Just pick out some of your favorite tunes, turn up the volume, and have some fun. After all, we are meant to be having fun in our lives.

Action Steps

Here are steps you can take to put these ideas into practice:

1. Select your favorite upbeat music.
2. Play this music every morning, between the time you wake and when you leave the house.
3. Have fun with it—sing and dance!

Singing in the Car

Another way I generated uplifting energy was to listen to songs on the radio when driving my car to work or other places. Often I would change the lyrics, and be spontaneous and just make up words (such as how I won the raffle and became a millionaire).

For instance, in the morning when I left my house, it was a fifteen to twenty-minute drive from my home to my workplace. My energy already was moving and shaking from the dancing at home. Since I wasn't able to dance in the car without becoming a public hazard, I limited myself to singing. When preparing for the raffle, I wanted to express in song that I had won the raffle and was a millionaire. Since I didn't know any songs with lyrics about being a millionaire, I decided that no matter what song played on the radio or my CD player, I would simply change the lyrics to fit my new wealth creation and make up words relating to my new status. You see, I was acting as if I had already won! I was feeling that my wish was already fulfilled.

If you've ever done improvisation, you know this is a good challenge. It can be tricky at first, but I just let it flow—kept the words coming, while laughing at myself and singing. The words involved my winning a million dollars and what I was doing with all the money: how was I spending it, saving it, donating money to various organizations, and making contributions in the world and in my community. Had another person been in the car with me (and be glad you weren't!), they might have thought I'd gone crazy. The verses didn't rhyme or even necessarily make sense, other than to convey that I had won a major raffle. My singing voice was not impressive (one would never guess I had been in the choir in elementary school), but I was having fun changing my energy and feeling totally happy. Invariably, I arrived at work with a big grin on my face. The people at work were much more serious, so I would tone things down a bit, but I was genuinely just happy.

Action Steps

Here are steps you can take to put these ideas into practice:

1. While listening to the music, make up your own words.

2. Create a story of what you want in life and sing it.

3. Remember be silly and have fun!

Write It Down

Writing typically was not something I would do on a regular basis. It was not comfortable for me at first, and it's amazing that now I am writing this book. It always seemed like I was too busy to write, and I was unsure of what to say or how to say it. I could sit and enjoy reading or thinking about various things or meditating. I just never wrote much, growing up or even in my later years, except for school papers or writing required for work proposals. In my television production work I would hire scriptwriters, so writing did not come as a natural way of expressing myself. I did, however, write down my vision for winning the raffle. I suppose I could have written more, to explain some of the details and experiences, but

I chose to do more of this in my visualizations.

Since then I have learned more about this process and acknowledge the power of writing things down (recording them electronically or on paper). Write about issues from your past; write about where you see yourself in the future (thirty days, ninety days, one year, or ten years from now); write about what you are dreaming of. What do the items on your wish list look like, feel like, taste and smell like? If, in my visualized future, I am living by the ocean, I would hear the sound of the ocean and see the waves and the beach. The sound helps me form a stronger picture in my mind, creating a more powerful visualization and imagination for the process.

Writing, like speaking, is a more powerful vibration than just thinking. While thinking certainly can be powerful, writing your dreams and visions helps clarify your focus on what you are declaring. Remember, you are not really asking for anything; it is yours already. Many spiritual teachers tell us that everything that is possible is already created—we just tune our attention and vibration to what it is we want, and the manifestation will happen when we are in alignment with our beliefs.

Writing will strengthen your conviction of purpose and engage your passion. I did feel the passion arise in me as I was writing things down; in fact I could feel that I started pressing harder with my pen and squeezing my hand tighter. I started writing faster and more determinedly, and could feel a stronger vibration throughout my body.

As much as I thought I didn't have time to write (and I didn't care for the process of writing at first), when I did sit down to write, the words and feelings started flowing. Many times I could barely keep up with my thoughts! I am now much better at writing, or at least more comfortable with the process. It has become easier to express myself and to want to share it.

So, start writing, and be as detailed as you can about who you are planning to be, and what you would like to have and experience in your life. Most of all, make it fun!

Action Steps

Here are steps you can take to put these ideas into practice:

1. Write down (on paper or using an electronic device) everything you want in life. Don't hold back; allow your imagination to run free and play. Remember that your imagination is the most powerful creative tool you have.

2. Spend a few minutes each morning writing down your goals and dreams, or do this in the evening before you go to sleep. Let your words and ideas melt into your subconscious as you sleep.

Imagination

Logic will get you from A to B. Imagination will take you anywhere.

~ Albert Einstein

Our greatest and most powerful possession is our imagination—we can dream anything we want at any time. There are no limits except our own limits of thought.

There is, however, a big difference between just letting our minds drift off into a dream or fantasy to play with (and perhaps discover things we might want, which is fun and exciting) and what could be termed *controlled imagination*. Controlled imagination is where you are focused and have a consistent and repetitive plan for a specific objective to manifest something you desire. If your imagination is uncontrolled and you lack the attention of the feeling of the wish you want fulfilled, you are just daydreaming, and your goals will be more difficult to reach. As the day moves on, you may not be focused in your imagination, but you can live in the feeling of the fulfillment of your wish.

How does one use controlled imagination? It's easy—simply employ your imagination to consistently focus on your desired end result and experience, and then feel the fulfillment of your wish, using as much intensity as you can. Be determined in your imagination! This is the way all creation happens.

Visualizing

When you visualize, you are using your imagination.

Visualizing yourself having the experience you intend to create can be a great tool for accomplishing the process of "Be, Do, and then Have."

Be the person you want to be, and **do** the things you would do if you were this person ("act as if"). If you are in alignment with your desire and beliefs, the universe will conspire on your behalf so that you will **have** or manifest your desire.

When I first started visualizing, it was not easy because I felt too connected or tied to my present reality and where I had been in the past. The more I learned about quantum physics, the more I realized that our present reality is only what we believe it to be.

The idea of "change your thoughts; change the world" started to really sink in. As I practiced daily, I began to see more details of my experience in the visualization of myself in a million-dollar house or having the money I won. This process initially can be a challenge, but after you have written your goals, intentions, and outcomes, it becomes easier. Make sure you first put this experience in writing, and the visualization process will become much easier.

The two most important things I learned from others about this process are to:

1. Visualize first, and then feel the feelings.

2. Go deeply into the details. Details help with the experience, but don't insist on them; just allow them to be a part of your experience. (If a blue Ferrari showed up instead of a red one, would you be good with that?) Identify and focus on your feelings of the end result. List as many details as you like, but don't attach to them. Play with the details and have fun with the process.

I cannot emphasize this enough: Elicit strong feelings about what you are creating—see the details and feel the feelings of that experience deeply (feel the joy, love, success, passion, and so forth).

For all the controllers and analytical types reading this, let go of the "how is it going to happen?" idea. You can no more control this process than you can control the weather. Just watch it develop and unfold.

By now, I had learned that experiencing would connect me with my passions. This is something I could not have done easily years earlier, but now I can laugh, love, and express my passion freely. I incorporated the feelings of happiness, joy, and success into my visualization of winning the raffle, seeing myself in the new house, or having the $1 million.

Here comes the tricky part of visualizing yourself as being the one who is experiencing the new reality: It is not as if you're watching a movie and you are in the movie (a third-person perspective). It's a first-person perspective, in which you experience being the star of your own movie. In my case, it was experiencing being inside my new home and living as a person with a $1million bank account. With the house or the money, I was looking, feeling, touching the objects, and greeting the people visiting me at my new home.

In these visualizations, we not only are in the movie, we are the movie. I was like an actor in the movie experiencing my new life, not a voyeur watching it. In my visualization I was walking around the house, preparing food, eating, and talking to visitors in the kitchen. Other activities included sitting or lying on the couch, playing pool in the recreation room, walking up the stairs to the bedroom, taking a shower, shaving in front of the bathroom mirror, and washing my hands in the sink. It took some practice to feel the emotional connection, but it became easier the more I practiced.

Consistent practice and repetition is crucial. Even if you don't feel connected at first, stay with it. The more you repeat this process daily and connect to it with feelings, the more the visualization will become natural and exciting. I was experiencing living in a home I had seen only in photographs, yet I had the knowing that it was mine.

My visualization included laughing and talking to people, and greeting them at the door. I felt like I lived there, and was happy and excited to be in that house. Since I had pictures of the house (they were posted on the website for the raffle), I could see all the details of the kitchen, living room, recreation room, bedrooms, bathrooms, and family room. At times I could feel the heat coming from the fireplace!

I downloaded the pictures to my cell phone and would look at them during the day, and also would access the website on my computer to see a larger display. The more I visualized, the easier it became to practice every day. And with the deeper connection came stronger feelings of being happy. This was no longer feeling like a distance fantasy; it felt real.

~~~

My process was to arise at five-thirty in the morning, take a shower, and then sit back on my bed or on a comfortable chair for twenty minutes and visualize. The process can be accomplished in as little as five minutes, so if you don't have much time, five minutes is fine.

The shower helped me wake up a bit, but not so much that my brain would be in high gear until I was on my way to work. In deep sleep our brainwaves are in the slow, delta state. As we awaken, our brainwaves quicken to the (still slow) theta state, which facilitates creativity and imagination. Children are almost continuously in the theta brainwave state for approximately the first five to seven years of their life, in which they are extremely creative and imaginative.

The next-faster brainwave state is alpha, which is characterized by deep relaxation and openness to suggestions. By not becoming too active too quickly, I allowed myself to stay in the alpha state, which is excellent for visualizing. The typical daily waking state of an adult is dominated by the faster beta brainwaves. Meditation and visualization are easier to accomplish when you already are in an alpha state (still relaxed after waking in the morning).

In the morning after awakening and in the evening just before sleep are good times to visualize. At these times our subconscious mind is more receptive to images and suggestions, and it works to place them in our consciousness and our "outer" reality.

When I close my eyes and visualize my new world, I make it colorful and include as many details as possible. And here is the most powerful part of any manifestation: I feel the experience of my new world. After five to ten minutes of visualizing, I'd have a big smile on my face and would pump my fist and yell, "Yes!" I had just been experiencing my new reality and felt elated. Our emotions deepen the seed of our experience. In fact, without emotions, we are only daydreaming. The emotion is the critical part.

Research at the Institute of Heartmath (a research and education organization dedicated to helping people reduce stress, self-regulate emotions, and build energy for healthy, happy lives) tells us that our heart is far stronger than our brain. Essentially, the heart is the boss of our brain. Our heart is constantly sending signals to our brain based on our feelings. Our emotions modulate the heart signal to the brain.

Our heart lets our brain know if we are happy, angry, fearful, or whatever emotion we are experiencing. The brain translates these signals, and then sends out messages in the form of hormones and chemicals to our cells and body. This is why our thoughts must be attached to our feeling-energy, because thoughts with no energy go nowhere.

Our outer world is a mirror of our inner world. When you work on creating your desired experience inside first, the outside world appears as you desire.

What was said to the rose that made it open,
was said to me,
here in my chest.

~ Rumi

Back to my plan: After my visualization, I would exercise, play an uplifting song, and sing and dance to the song. At this point it was only six-thirty in the morning, and already I was beaming and bouncing around the house.

It felt so good! This feeling would carry me through the day. I might be very busy at work, with meetings to attend, calls to make, and reports to prepare, but I was calm and felt happy. I enjoyed my work, the people, and my day.

So, are you ready to begin now?

Action Steps

Here are steps you can take to put these ideas into practice:

1. Sit in a quiet place and let your imagination focus on an area of your life where you want to create something new. Spend about five minutes each day on this activity.

2. Focus on only one area at a time.

3. Spend a few minutes getting a vision of what it looks like, and then move into the feeling of it.

4. Feel it, as if your wish is fulfilled at this present moment.

5. Stay connected with that feeling as long as you can, as you go about your day.

Vision Boards

The Universe is not looking at your vision board;
the universe is responding to your feelings.

A vision board is another great tool, one I use myself. It can be used in tandem with your visualization process. To create a physical board, start with a large piece of poster board. Look for pictures to paste on it that represent the person you want to be, places you want to go, the types of people you want to be with, and experiences you want to have. Use these images to help guide your thoughts and feelings to make sure you are connected with your feelings when you are looking at the vision board.

Please be aware that just putting images on the board will not necessarily bring these things into your reality. The universe is not looking at your vision board; the universe is responding to your feelings of the images as you are experiencing them. Remember that it's all about the vibration or energy you are feeling—and the universe responds to that feeling.

Again, it is important to put yourself into these images and experience the feeling of *you* in these settings. Don't just watch yourself being the person in the image—feel everything you would be feeling, using all your senses as if you were in that place or having that experience.

Meditation

When we meditate, our brainwaves change. During meditation, the balance of the brainwave activity in the human brain shifts. There is less activity of beta waves (the thinking and stress-related brainwave) and more activity of alpha and theta brainwaves (the relaxation brainwaves).

As this shift occurs, our brainwaves stimulate more happiness and contentment, which affects our perception of daily activities. This state of happiness or contentment may last a few hours or a few days. When we meditate, our positive emotions increase—we become more intuitive and more relaxed. In meditation, as we purposely slow down or stop our mind chatter even temporarily, we also stop or slow down any negative or resistive thoughts regarding what we choose to be or what we desire.

The reason many of us struggle with manifesting the things we truly desire is that there seems to be a constant battle between our positive, joyful, and desired states and our programmed, habitual, nonproductive, or negative beliefs, doubts, and habits. When our joyful and happy states of mind are more consistent and positive than any negative states of mind we may have, progress is made, and manifestation is much easier and quicker.

I have been meditating for many years, and I have good days and not-so-good days in my practice. It isn't what happens in your practice on any given day that matters; it is the cumulative benefit over a period of time. This is called the *compound effect.* The compound effect works in every area of your life, especially when you are looking to create new habits and make significant changes in your life. It works in your spiritual, physical, financial, social, and psychological state. When you consistently perform certain tasks (even for short periods), the compound effects can be massive, especially if you are consistent and dedicated to the endeavor. Financier Warren Buffet created his billions by doing this, and bodybuilder Charles Atlas went from a skinny type to the most popular muscleman of his time.

It works best to begin with short meditation periods, perhaps just five minutes a day. After awhile, double it to ten minutes a day. If you meditated for ten minutes every day, you would see benefits in your life very soon. The changes may be subtle, but there will be a difference. The energy of your body will be different and people will notice, perhaps even before you notice a difference. People like being around energy that is calm and at ease.

If meditation is new to you, remember to not judge yourself or rate how your mediation is on a given day—was it good or not good? It is all good; it's just sometimes our mind is more distracted and more difficult to quiet down. I've been meditating for the past fifteen years and I still have days where it is hard to quiet my mind. It doesn't happen as often as it used to, but if there are many things going on in my outside world, my inside world is also very active and feels a bit out of control. I just return to focusing on my breath. In addition, I use a meditation CD, which helps a great deal.

I meditate for at least ten minutes every morning and sometimes for twenty minutes. If I have a short amount of time on a particular morning, I'll just sit for five minutes. It makes a positive difference in the entire day.

Action Steps

Here are steps you can take to put these ideas into practice:

1. Be seated, and be still and quiet. Focus on your breathing.

2. As thoughts arise, gently let them go.

3. If you are new at meditating, start with a five-minute meditation. As you feel ready, extend it for longer periods

4. Other options are to take a meditation class or listen to a guided meditation recording.

Gratitude: The Acts and Thoughts of Appreciation

A daily practice of gratitude may be the most important practice of all that I've listed. I recently heard someone say that without gratitude, there can be no happiness. This makes perfect sense: How can you be happy if you don't feel grateful for and appreciate all that you have in your life? It could be a beloved person, your health, family, work and career, home, friends, hobbies, and everything else that brings you joy and contentment. Maybe you would like some things to be different, but anyone can find reasons to be grateful for many wonderful things in their life.

In the teachings of Abraham from Esther Hicks, this is what Abraham says about appreciation or gratitude:

Love and appreciation are identical vibrations. Appreciation is the vibration of alignment with who-you-are. Appreciation is the absence of everything that feels bad and the presence of everything that feels good. When you focus upon what you want—when you tell the story of how you want your life to be—you will come closer and closer to the vicinity of appreciation, and when you reach it, it will pull you toward all things that you consider to be good in a very powerful way.

~ Abraham

The challenge for many is that they tend to focus on the negative aspects of their lives—the problems and things that aren't working. Yet, there are so many more things that are working, that are going well, that do make our lives better and more satisfying! It isn't hard to identify these things and feel appreciation for them.

Research consistently shows that people who express gratitude and appreciation not only feel better about their lives overall, they are more optimistic about the future and have fewer health problems than average. Compared to people that don't, people that use gratitude journals reportedly are more satisfied with their lives, fall asleep more quickly and easily, and feel more refreshed in the morning when they wake up.

Health researchers at the University of Connect-icut conducted a study of people that had experienced one heart attack. Patients who recognized benefits and gains from their heart attack (such as a greater appreci-ation for life) had a lower-than-average risk of a second heart attack.

If you are unaccustomed to appreciating and feeling grateful for things in your life, place some visual cues around your home to remind you to appreciate certain things. Another good idea is to have gratitude partner, someone who you can share with on a regular basis about good things that are happening for you. With modern technology, you can text, tweet, or email friends and family about things you appreciate. The more you express your appreciation and gratitude, the happier you will feel.

If you find yourself complaining about someone or something, stop and remind yourself of something to be grateful for instead.

It's easy to be grateful for the big things that happen in our lives (a new job, a new home, a new partner) while overlooking the small, day-to-day joys that we tend to take for granted. Why not be grateful for benefits like indoor plumbing, hot and cold water, central heating, and having clothes and shoes? Most of us have a vehicle that gets us from point A to point B, and we are able to drive on paved roads to commute to work. Living in Colorado, I see mountains every day when I go out, and I appreciate their majestic, beauty, and the way clouds form around them. There is so much beauty in nature, trees, birds, wild animals, and pets! The list for me goes on and on.

Stop for a moment and write down all the things you are grateful for, both big and small. You'll see that the list could be endless. How about being grateful for the people that built your car or your home, or those that designed and crafted your shoes, furniture, or artwork? Spend at least ten minutes on this exercise, and I can almost guarantee that you'll notice a change in your feelings immediately. Gratitude is a powerful feeling.

While you are writing down what you are presently grateful for, why not take it a step further and be grateful for the things you are about to receive? You may not know exactly what they are, so use your imagination to create things you want to experience, and then be grateful for their arrival into your reality. This practice will help create a greater feeling of abundance. Once you begin to connect with the feelings, the manifestations start occurring.

Gratitude Journal

If you don't have a gratitude journal, start one. A gratitude journal is a great way to spend some time every day writing down the things you were grateful for on that particular day. Because writing is more powerful than just thinking, it has a stronger vibration and can have more powerful effects.

Certainly you can write things at any time of the day, but I suggest writing in your journal every evening before going to sleep. This practice is particularly powerful for several reasons. First, it's a good way to recapture your day and focus on things you were especially grateful for. Second, it puts you in a positive frame of mind. Third, the thoughts we think just before falling asleep tend to be present in our subconscious mind all night while we sleep.

What kinds of thoughts do you want to have before you fall asleep? Would you prefer loving thoughts, or do you want to be thinking about the things that went wrong during the day or the horrible stories that were on the evening news? I stopped watching the news for this very reason.

The thoughts we have before we go to sleep tend

to penetrate our subconscious mind. Given the power of our subconscious mind, we have no idea what it could create for us the next day or the next week! Our thoughts send subtle messages to our subconscious mind, and these messages have an impact. And even more so, our thoughts have an associated vibration in the form of feelings.

In general, it's best to have positive thoughts and feelings all day long, but it's most important before sleep. At that time, we want to make sure to direct our gratitude and appreciation to our subconscious mind.

Action Steps

Here are steps you can take to put these ideas into practice:

1. Keep a gratitude journal at your bedside.

2. Every night, write down five to seven things you are especially grateful for on that day.

3. Connect with the feelings of gratitude for the things you have documented.

Exercise: Let's Get Physical

*We should consider every day lost on which
we have not danced at least once.*

~Friedrich Nietzsche

You won't change your energy by sitting on a chair or lying on a couch—you have to get out and move. Since everything in the universe is energy, your energy in motion helps to create or manifest your intention. In this case, your intention is to create greater happiness.

So, let's move your body! A great way to get the energy flowing throughout your body is to stretch, walk, jog, or do some form of exercise. Even sitting and doing deep breathing for ten minutes is a form of inner movement and relaxation. So whenever you feel shut down, hopeless, or fearful, move and uplift your body as a way to move stuck energy. Here are some suggestions:

- Take a quick walk, even if it's just around the room or down the hallway and back.

- Walk or run up and down a flight of stairs.

- Bend, twist, and stretch.

- Do a set of pushups, jumping jacks, or squats.

- Go outside and experience the weather, whatever it is, just for a minute or two.

- Close your eyes and listen to the sounds of wind, birds, insects, or rain.

- Look at or touch a living plant or tree, indoors or outdoors.

- Dance—anywhere and anytime.

As Friedrich Nietzsche, the German philosopher, said, "We should consider every day lost on which we have not danced at least once."

A great thing to do (and what I do) is to play good dance music and dance around the house. It can be only one song, and you don't have to dance for hours. Of course, you also could go to a club to listen to music and dance. If you don't feel you are good dancer, then stay home and dance by yourself or with a partner. This definitely will get your energy moving. Did you ever notice how much better you dance when no one is watching? When free of concern for what others are thinking, you are able to better express yourself.

This is how I would start my day every morning: I would play fun, upbeat music, and dance around the living room. If you do this first thing in the morning, you can set your energy level for the day. I noted that it was important to get out of one's comfort zone, and this is one of the best ways to do that. Let loose and be silly, and you'll be laughing in no time as well! Laughing at yourself while you are dancing is a great practice.

Also, exercise is considered a "keystone" habit, in that it has a ripple effect on many other areas of our lives. The positive effects are both physical and mental. For instance, people that exercise frequently generally have (or develop) better eating habits, and they also sleep better. Exercise strengthens the cardiovascular system and enhances brain functioning through the release of serotonin and other neurotransmitters. These brain chemicals not only make us feel better, they decrease stress and enhance productivity.

There are numerous books and articles available that detail the positive effects of exercise, so I won't go into all the benefits here—but trust me, the list goes on! I have been active my whole life, and some form of exercise always has been a part of my lifestyle. You don't have to spend hours in a gym or out competing to get these benefits; thirty minutes a day is all you need. If your schedule doesn't allow for thirty minutes of exercise, then do at least ten minutes. The important thing is to do something! You can start at any age, from almost any physical condition, and you will see a difference.

If you don't presently have an exercise plan, commit

today to start one. Make a list of the things that interest you and get started! (People with significant health issues should discuss a new fitness program with a healthcare practitioner as appropriate, of course.)

Action Steps

Here are steps you can take to put these ideas into practice:

1. Every day, do something to get your energy moving, even if it's only for 5 or 10 minutes.

2. Every other day, set aside a longer period of time, like 20 to 30 minutes

3. Once a week, do some form of exercise for one hour.

There are many other ways to change your vibration and expand your joy and happiness. Here are more ideas:

Eat healthy food, take baths, journal, read spiritual books or books that make you feel better, play more, get out in nature, go for walks in a garden or park, spend time at the ocean or in the mountains, spend time with animals or children, hang out with friends, go window shopping, clear out clutter, have more sex, watch inspiring movies, work on a creative project, watch sunrises and sunsets, travel, learn new things, take deep breaths, laugh, and just do whatever makes you feel better.

~ ~ ~

True happiness... is not attained through self-gratification,
but through fidelity to a worthy purpose.

~Helen Keller

Chapter 6

PURPOSE

———

What is your purpose? Why are you doing anything? Why do you want to continue doing what you are doing? Why is your future important?

A list of such questions can go on and on.

Your purpose—the reason you want to do something—could be the most important question you may never have answered for yourself. Why do anything? We don't always have to know *how* something will be done, but it's important to know the *why*. This is the first thing to identify. (In this section, I am using the words *why* and *purpose* interchangeably.)

Why be happy? Why not be happy? If you could choose any emotion, I would think that being happy would be near the top of your list.

For thousands of years, great writers, philosophers, and spiritual leaders have been telling us that the external world is created from our internal world. If you don't like your outside world, change yourself, and then watch the outside world change before your eyes.

When I was growing up, it seemed that the only answer I ever received when I asked "Why?" was, "Because I told you so." This answer usually came from people in authority. I didn't take ownership of my *why*; I didn't have my own reason. You probably would agree that there isn't much motivation involved in the "because I told you so" scenario.

Often I did things out of fear: the fear that I would be punished if I didn't obey rules or comply with authority. The threatened punishments ranged from burning in hell for eternity (from the Catholic Church) to being grounded by my parents.

Typically I used other people's *whys*, so I didn't create many of my own. Early in life I had some smaller *whys*, such as doing work to earn spending money. I played sports in order to get noticed, and after awhile it was important to me to be athletic. But the big reason why—my purpose—was missing.

I had set up a life and lifestyle based on doing things. At first it entailed doing what I was told by others; later, it was doing what I told myself. I didn't examine my life as well as I could have. The big dreams were not there, and so the big *why* and my life purpose was also absent.

When I started my business at age twenty-five, I had a purpose, but I also had a lot of fears. It became a battle of the *whys* versus the fears, and the fears were winning. Later I realized that the *why* is much more powerful than any fears. No matter how far away the goal appears or how hard it may seem to reach it, if your reason why is big enough and you believe in it strongly enough—and consistently move in the direction of it—you can achieve anything.

Do you have a *why*? If not, that's okay, but now is the time to create one, and make it big! There's no point in playing small, or even medium-scale. To quote an adage, "Shoot for the moon. Even if you miss, you'll land among the stars."

Take some time to think about your purpose: an hour or even a few days. Identifying your purpose is the first step for creating greater happiness in your life. When we have purpose, we come from a happier state. We take actions because they have value and meaning.

Moving toward your goal may be challenging at times, but you can be happy knowing that you are moving in the direction of your dreams. This alone can bring you happiness.

Remember the words of Lao Tzu: "A journey of a thousand miles begins with a single step."

When your purpose is big enough—and when you believe in it—you can move mountains.

Many times when I did have a bigger dream or bigger purpose, my fear became stronger and I abandoned my dream. That's why I feel it is important to look for small steps, goals, and wins along the way, so that you can see your progress. And, know that the bigger goal just lies ahead.

Connect with your purpose and feel really good about it! Now, you have direction and are not living your life in default or moving aimlessly. Live and move in the direction of your life—with purpose.

~ ~ ~

*If we're growing, we're always going to be
out of our comfort zone.*

~ John Maxwell

Chapter 7

GET OUT OF YOUR COMFORT ZONE

———

"Life begins at the end of your comfort zone." When I read this quote from Neale Donald Walsch a few years ago, I really connected with it because I knew I had just experienced this. I have been to the edge of my comfort zone many times, but always came back to the safer place. I felt safer, but actually it wasn't safer: It was where I kept all my fears and worries. I kept coming back to the safe zone because it seemed scarier and more fearful to change. I wanted to change myself, but I didn't know how.

There is a beautiful quote that says, "Just as the caterpillar thought its life was over, it became a butterfly." How much better could this be stated as it relates to our own life? We spend years (at least our first few years—literally) crawling around, getting to know ourselves, experiencing and feeling comfortable with our surroundings. Sometimes we like the life we are living and sometimes we want to experience something more, but our comfort zone holds us back. It keeps us limited and traps us in a cocoon, where we don't emerge to our true potential: the vibrant and amazing human beings that we are.

I believe that everyone really wants to emerge from the cocoon and fly, yet we don't know how, and are afraid to even try. We wonder, what will it look like—what will we look like? It may be a little messy or disorganized the first, but so what? Open up to the world and spread your wings, and the world will open up to you. As motivational speaker Les Brown would say, "Leap, and grow your wings on the way down."

Learning something new always take some practice. Expanding who you are and what you can do is like learning a new language, driving a car for the first time, riding a bike, learning to swim, or even learning to walk. Back when you were learning to walk, you didn't give up just because you fell down time and time again!

It was part of the process.

For some reason, when we become adults, we think that falling down or making mistakes is a bad thing. Let's clear this up right now—it's not! The biggest mistake we make is not trying new things and having new experiences, and therefore going nowhere. If you want to get somewhere other than where you are, make peace with feeling vulnerable and (temporarily) awkward. Remember that life is about learning and growing and becoming more, and the only way to become more is to try new things and move out of your comfort zone.

Our comfort zones keep us trapped. They contain us like a cocoon, but we have to break free of the cocoon to fly—and fly we must. The bu tterfly does not crawl around very well; it spreads its wings and takes flight. Even the butterfly, if it stays in one place too long, doesn't have an optimum experience. Its natural predators may attack it, so the butterfly needs to keep moving, keep flying. We too need to keep growing, or "predators" like laziness, fear and worry, isolation, or poor health will catch up with us. Remember that staying in our comfort zone keeps us from becoming more of who we can be.

In the movie *Groundhog Day*, Bill Murray's character awakens each day to the same situation. Once he figured out how his life was working, he made the most of each day and learned and grew—and yes, even he became a new person, a much better person.

Such a change doesn't happen overnight, but when we take steps each day, before we realize it, we are flying. We've moved out past the end of our comfort zone to experience something new, fun, and exhilarating.

When I started my journey to create greater happiness, I felt more alive every day, as I moved a little further out of my comfort zone. Some days I took smaller steps; some days I made bigger leaps, but I kept moving. As you will discover, the end of your comfort zone is a moving target: You never stay in the same place for long; it moves as you move. There is no end, only progress toward a goal of living more happily. Being happy does not have an end. It's not like a football game where the end zone is a fixed position and once you have reached that place, you've won some points. In getting out of your comfort zone and creating greater happiness, you score points all the time.

Life and the universe are always expanding, and we have a choice to expand and grow with it. We can increase our joy, love, and happiness every day by pushing the limits of our comfort zone.

So try something different—go to the edge of your comfort zone and take a leap.

When you have come to the edge of all light that you know and are about to drop off into the darkness of the unknown, faith is knowing one of two things will happen: There will be something solid to stand on, or you will be taught to fly.

~ Patrick Overton

What if there was more and greater happiness, and it just kept getting bigger and bigger? This is what happens when we keep pushing the edge of our comfort zone. There is always more, and it's up to us to choose to have more, to be more, to experience more, to feel more, and to live more. The more we feel motivated to have joy in our life, the more joy we will feel in life.

What did I do to get out of my comfort zone? To start with, I changed my habits.

~~~

Take care of your Thoughts
because they become Words.

Take care of your Words
because they will become Actions.

Take care of your Actions
because they will become Habits.

Take care of your Habits
because they will form your Character.

Take care of your Character
because it will form your Destiny,
and your Destiny will be your Life.

~Unknown

Chapter 8

HABITS

———

What are habits, and what meaning do they have in our lives? What do our habits tell us about ourselves?

Definition of a *habit*: A settled or regular tendency or practice, especially one that is hard to give up. The prevailing disposition or character of a person's thoughts and feelings. An acquired mode of behavior that has become nearly or completely involuntary. A behavior pattern acquired by frequent repetition or physiologic exposure that shows itself in regularity or increased facility of performance.

Just reading the definition makes me more aware of the power of our habits. The good news is that at least we now know what we are dealing with. And in my experience, the better I understand the situation I am in, the better I can create a plan to resolve it.

Our habits tell us a lot about who we are. In fact, we *are* our habits: Good, bad or indifferent, we are what we do on a regular and consistent basis.

Are you even aware of your habits? Do you understand the power they wield in your life?

Scientific research tells us that 95 to 97 percent of what we do on a daily basis is a habit. That doesn't leave much room for our conscious awareness, does it?

Our habits come from our subconscious mind. Science tells us that our subconscious mind is up to one million times stronger and faster than our conscious mind. This fact alone should make us think about our habits more seriously.

Habits are mostly based on our beliefs, and our beliefs are stories we tell ourselves. Your story may have originated from another person (from someone saying or doing something to you), but you must have taken it on as your belief, which formed the habit. We form habits through our thoughts and words, and by our actions.

Habits can take us on a path we might not welcome, like eating foods that are not healthy for us, using negative self talk, not exercising (although you know it's one of the best things you can do for your overall health), or not smiling enough. If we want to make changes in our lives, examining our habits is one of the first places to start.

Certainly all habits are not bad; some are very useful as we go through our daily lives. Useful habits include driving a car, tying our shoes, and performing repetitive daily tasks. These habits save our brain a lot of energy, making it available for doing other processing.

If our habits and beliefs are preventing us from living our lives to the fullest and becoming happier, then we have a problem. We need to create a new set of beliefs and habits. This starts with new thoughts, words, and actions.

When I was about ten years old, in the fifth grade, I thought I heard a teacher of mine talking to my mother, telling her that I was an average student. This had an impact on me, because I then believed I was an average person. I didn't want to be an average person, but I began to believe I was. Of course, I could have reacted to that idea in other ways, but I felt that I needed to try harder because I didn't think I was smart enough.

My grades usually were above average, and I did especially well in math, but there was always something inside me that said, "Maybe I'm not smart enough." That thought also could be interpreted as, "Maybe I'm not good enough."

~~~

What about our habits in relation to others—our opinions, attitudes, and beliefs about other people? Do we accept everyone as they are, or are we forming opinions based on our previous experience, which has become a habit? This could be done by deciding something about a person based on the way they look or dress, their race or coloring, if they wear a uniform, or any of a myriad of external characteristics.

Our beliefs form our subconscious habits, and many of these can be way off-base from reality. They may be founded in a childhood experience, or perhaps something from our recent past. Regardless of when it occurred, we still carry that belief today. It has become a subconscious habit. Maybe the belief is keeping us from starting a business, succeeding at a business, or simply having a conversation with a stranger. Beliefs come in all shapes, sizes, and flavors.

In the past I sometimes formed opinions about people based on the way they looked, and sometimes even resisted meeting them. Yet when I finally did meet the person, often they turned out to be interesting, smart, and fun—and I greatly appreciated the experience with them.

Our habits and patterns of behavior can constrain us and limit our experiences. I have so many great and wonderful conversations now with people everywhere. All I have to do is start a casual conversation with them (it could be in a store, at an event, in a parking lot, or anywhere). I have turned it into a fun challenge to see whom can I meet every day, and to smile and even laugh with them. It helps everyone, and can have a ripple effect that is like a "gift that keeps on giving."

In creating habits, for us to experience a happier life, we need to express and share who we are with others and allow others to do the same for us. If we carry around a belief that we are not good enough, smart enough, attractive enough, or capable enough, how are we going to live to our highest potential?

I don't feel that where or how I learned a pattern of behavior is as important as simply changing my behavior in the direction of my choice. However, at times I realize that looking back at my past and understanding why I am doing something can be a very valuable process. What is important is that we decide to make a change and move in that direction, and that we are persistent and consistent in our new direction. This is the way habits form and change takes place. There really aren't any shortcuts to this process.

The only other way a significant change takes place is if we have a sudden insight or awareness that creates a change in our lives. This sudden awareness could be due to an unpleasant experience, such as a divorce or health problem, or (on the positive side) it could be an apparent miracle, or a mystical experience such as a visit from an angel.

Changing a habit takes consistent commitment over an extended period of time. We can see changes over a period of a few weeks, but remember that we want to create a long-term change. If the new habit is changing a long-standing pattern, it likely will take more effort and a longer period. Some research shows that we'll start to see a new pattern in twenty-one days. Other research says it can take ninety days to solidify a new habit.

If you are creating fun new habits, the time required need not be of great concern because you will be doing things and making changes that are fun. Wouldn't you want to continue these enjoyable new habits for the rest of your life?

~~~

If you feel you are holding yourself back with a particular belief and habit, ask yourself, why do I believe this? What story am I telling myself that supports this habit?

Change your habit to support you, and to help you become who you want to be. If you're not sure what habits are holding you back, ask someone else: a family member, friend, coworker, therapist, or life coach. I'm sure you will get an answer. It may not be what you wanted to hear, but it may be just what you needed and likely will appear at just the right time.

Some habits can be very easy to change; others may be more of a challenge, but it's all worth the effort. People have transformed their entire lives by changing their habits and patterns of behavior. Corporations have changed and become more successful by teaching new habits and energizing a workforce. I certainly changed my level of happiness by creating several new habits.

Remember that we are not locked into our beliefs or habits. Perhaps we lack the willpower or feel a bit lazy, but our brain is very capable of learning, changing, growing, and adapting. It is really our choice, and there is no better time to start than *right now*!

Because you always did something a certain way in the past does not mean it must be that way in the future. Your past determines your future only if you allow it to. And yes, old dogs can learn new tricks! And you are not a dog.

If you don't like a behavior or thought that you have, cancel the old one (mentally, at first), and learn a new one. You cannot create new habits by blaming, complaining, or condemning. This applies to you or anyone else in your life. Take full responsibility and create the life you believe you can have. This is why beliefs are so important: You can only become what you believe you can. When you limit your beliefs, you limit your life. Take a look at your beliefs: How big are they? They can be as big or small as you choose. Do you believe you have limits, or are you capable of anything you choose?

This is where your imagination comes in, as I discussed in the Visualizing section of Chapter 5. Use your imagination to expand your ideas of who you think you are and who you can become.

I like to constantly learn and try new things; the novelty keeps my life interesting. And yes, I have to get out of my comfort zone many times to do this, which is not always easy at first, but I know it's good for me. When I do get out of my comfort zone, the new endeavor usually is a lot more fun than I thought it would be. The fear is simply the apprehension of doing something new, but the act of actually doing something different is enjoyable. Often it feels a little awkward to do something new for the first time, but then it becomes a new skill or an artistic expression that you can quickly learn (perhaps even master) and just have fun with.

Let's not leave *fun* out of the equation. In spite of what seems to be a general idea in the world of seriousness and fear, *fun* should be our top priority. Go out one day with the intention to just have fun—get out of your comfort zone and let go. It could be one of the best days you've ever had!

When I find myself in an uncomfortable situation or notice that I seem to keep doing the same things over and over, I start asking questions: What would it be like if I did something different, or just improved upon what I was doing, taking it to a new level? What if I acted differently, thought differently, or learned something different? When I wanted to try a different type of exercise (different from my typical running, biking, or being in the gym or yoga studio), I decided to try a triathlon (a swimming, biking, and running event). It turned out to be a great workout and more fun than biking or running alone.

Learning is a great way to keep our brains active. When we learn new things, our brains grow and change. Our brain is activated and the neurotransmitter dopamine is released into the cells, energizing both the brain and the body.

Start Small

When changing your habits, it's important to set yourself up for success. We do that by setting smaller, shorter-range goals at first. We may have a big goal in mind at the end, but should focus on things that are easier to accomplish at first. And reward yourself along the way for accomplishing your smaller goals. This gives you the opportunity to feel good about yourself and what you are doing. And, know that there is light at the end of the tunnel!

Whether it is climbing a mountain peak, running a marathon, or getting a PhD, look for goals and successes along the way. Identify points where you can measure your progress, enabling you to enjoy, the entire journey. Choose a goal you can reach in a week, a month, or a semester. This allows you to look back on your progress and quickly see that you have made a difference in your life, and perhaps in the lives of others. Do not underestimate the power you have and your influence on others when you make changes in your life.

If you've seen the movie, *It's a Wonderful Life*, with Jimmy Stewart, you know what I mean. I watch this movie every year because I feel that what I do with my life is affecting of others' lives. I certainly want that effect to be positive, even if I don't know what it is or who I am having an effect on. We have more power than we realize. So get out there and make some changes in many lives, including your own! Start with your life, and you never know whose lives will be changed and impacted along the way.

When I was training for my first triathlon a few years ago, I had been a runner for many years and had been biking longer distances for several years, but had not been swimming in a long time. I practiced in the pool, and that was going fine. However, the big challenge came when I did my first open-water practice swim and looked at the half-mile distance in the lake. I could not believe it at first—it was so much longer than I had expected. A half-mile in the pool is a lot of short laps, plus you can touch the bottom and pull over to the side of the pool to rest. When you are driving a car, a half-mile seems like no distance at all. The open water was a little scary for me. I knew how to swim and had a wetsuit, so I wasn't concerned about drowning. I simply was not sure I could swim that distance. Although I had swum the distance in the pool, fear now seemed to take control.

My goal for the open-water swim was just to finish the practice. I didn't care how long it took or what I looked like; I just wanted to be able to swim the half-mile course. It was hard at first, and the difficulty was mostly psychological. There were some buoys along the way, so I focused on getting to the next buoy, and then the next one. This made the swim much easier.

The more I practiced, the easier it became, and then I started to enjoy it. At that point I began to challenge myself: to go a little faster and work more on my form, so that I would burn less energy and be more efficient in the water. I took a triathlon swim lesson, and this helped. After doing the first three triathlons, I looked forward to the swim portion of the race more than the biking and running portions.

Learning to be happy is also a skill. First you make the choice to begin, get committed and disciplined, and then start a process of learning the habits and skills that are required.

The same principles apply to learning almost any new

skill. At first it feels awkward and uncomfortable, and you wonder, *why am I doing this?* But the more you practice, the easier it gets and the more enjoyable it becomes. Before long, you completely forget the struggles you went through. You find yourself enjoying the progress you make and focusing on doing even better.

Chemical Reactions

One of the main reasons changing some of our habits can be challenging is that there is a chemical component to our habits. Science tells us that for every feeling we have, there is a chemical process taking place, and we become "addicted" to that chemical infusion into our brain and bloodstream.

There is a chemical response in our brains and the cells of our body for every feeling we have: love, fear, worry, anger, victimization, happiness, and so forth. And the more we are connected to the feelings we have on a daily basis, the more likely we will continue to support those feelings, even if they are in opposition to what we really want. We don't want to feel angry, but we keep doing it every day, so it becomes easy to do it over and over. We want to smile, but the frown on our face keeps showing up. It affects us negatively and also impacts others around us.

Looking back at my life years ago, I can see that I often perceived myself to be a victim. Now it is apparent that I was "addicted" to that feeling of victimization. Although I didn't like it, I was comfortable with the feeling, and that made it harder to change my behavior. However, the more determined I became to change, the easier it was to change the feeling.

The synapses in our brain, a network of communication between our nerve cells and the patterns they create, correspond to our habits. The more frequent and stronger our habits are, the more the pathway for the synapses becomes open and creates a strong, predictable pattern. Our habits become like an old road in a forest where the tire tracks or ruts are deep, and sometimes grass won't grow there. It's a trail that has been traveled many, many times over many years. It becomes the path of least resistance, and that path will get deeper and deeper over time.

I remember when I was growing up in Michigan, after we had a big snowfall, because of the humidity and the cold, the snow would freeze. On the streets, the car tires would create deep grooves. These grooves would become so deep (six to twelve inches) that when someone's tires were in the grooves, it was almost impossible to get them out. It took a lot of engine power (and sometimes people pushing the car) to get out of the groove so you could turn onto your driveway or another street.

With habits, the routes in our brain become like the deep grooves on Michigan roads. We create the grooves, which are the pathways of our thoughts and feelings. We become so entrenched in our ways of thinking and feeling that we have to dig our way out of the old path to create a new path. But once the new path is created, it becomes our new habit, and the old path becomes the path less traveled.

The main point is to focus on the new habits you are creating. Yes, we are trying to change old habits, but it's where you place your intention that is important. Put your intention on the direction you are going. It is said that the reason that vehicles' rearview mirror is so small and the windshield so big is that we are meant to focus on where are going and not on where we've been. Our future is before us! Don't pull the past into your present, because the present becomes your future.

When I was working on creating a happier life for myself, I wasn't focusing on the areas I wanted to change. I was focusing on where I wanted to go and who I wanted to be. As a result, I created more happiness in my life, and my fear and worry began fading away.

What I Learned in the Process

The process I undertook to raise my vibration and create greater happiness was the most significant endeavor I've ever taken on. Writing a book about the experience was another project, and a challenge in itself. I was able to relive the "creating happiness" process by explaining it to my readers and by continuing to deeply commit myself to further my journey and self-discovery.

But this process has given me more than just greater joy and happiness. Even more significant was the letting go of fear and worry that had consumed so much of my life experience. I am a different person in many respects, in ways that are difficult to describe. I shifted to a different reality, in which new doors have opened and opportunities to experience even greater joy have surfaced. By changing my inner world, my "outer" experience of the world changed.

During the past two years I have also experience a deeper love for myself, for others, and for all of life I have greater appreciation for people in all walks of life.

Challenges in life don't go away, but how I respond

to them has changed. I am no longer reacting or having a subconscious response, as would occur in previous challenges. It seems that I created a new thought pattern or neural network in my brain, one that responds to opportunities and challenges in a very different way than it did before.

I realize that I can create another vision or aspect of myself to explore. Yes, it takes some work, as learning any new skill does. That's really not so bad.

The challenges I have chronicled in this book may have been the most significant ones I will face. Addressing them led to a profound, foundational change. And now that the foundation has been reset and strengthened, I can start building, adding new floors and levels and continuing to climb. Since I don't mind climbing stairs, there may be no limit to how far I can go!

It is as if I found a spark inside me and ignited a fire, and the fire continues to build. I almost have no choice but to let it spread to others. For instance, I'm expanding my speaking career and planning seminars to help others discover the gifts that live inside them.

Perhaps this book has ignited that spark in you! We all have the spark; it is inside every one of us. The spark is your higher self, waiting for you to rekindle your passion. If you haven't started to follow my suggestions and ideas to raise your vibration and create more joy and happiness for yourself, is my sincerest intent and desire that you start today. Of all the exercises I covered, meditation may seem like the only one that is focused inwardly. The others may seem like activities to do on the outside. However, there is much more going on than may be apparent when we perform these activities. Our brain chemistry changes and so do the cells, organs, and body systems.

The universe is operating at a higher frequency than Earth has been in the past. As we raise our vibration, we become more aligned with the universe, the source of all things. From this higher vibration, we see and experience the world with a new awareness.

You may notice subtle changes at first; they can be gradual, and some may be difficult to detect. Following a daily practice is important. Recently, a few weeks after being interviewed about my upcoming book on a radio show, I had the uplifting experience of hearing from one of the listeners. The man had started practicing my exercises daily, and he noticed significant changes in the first few weeks! These exercises will work for most everyone.

Remember that happiness is a choice—every moment

of every day, you can choose how you will feel and experience yourself and the world around you. Decide it, demand it, feel it, express it, and live it! Know that it is yours if you desire it. Be determined, dedicated, and consistent. Use your imagination, along with everything else you've learned, to be happy now.

Know that you are more than you may think you are! The life you desire may simply require a change in your beliefs about yourself and who you can become.

~ ~ ~

I look forward to hearing about your progress.
Please contact me through my website,
www.JamesRAnderson.net.

Wishing you a happy life!

James

ABOUT THE AUTHOR

James Anderson is an award-winning film and video producer and director, professional speaker, entrepreneur, and happiness-seeker. His first book, "Creating Happiness," was inspired after two decades of study in spiritual teachings, personal growth, and the Law of Attraction. His mission and passion is to help others connect with their innate happiness. James discovered and created a set of habits that he used to transform his life—habits that will work for anyone. He believes happiness and joy are our natural states, and that we can build new skills and habits to raise our vibration and access these states.

Happiness is a choice—and when we choose happiness, our lives change, and fears and worries begin to fade away. James lives in Denver, Colorado, and enjoys keeping active and healthy with yoga, meditation, hiking, skiing, snowshoeing, and participating in triathlons.

Recommended Reading

———

Wishes Fulfilled, by Dr. Wayne Dyer, ISBN: 1401937276

Life Visioning, by Machael Bernard Beckwith, ISBN: 1604076291

The Power of Awareness, by Neville Goddard, ISBN-10: 1453698787

The Secret, by Rhonda Byrne , ISBN-10: 1582701709,

Law of Attraction Made Simple, Magnetize Your Heartfelt Desires, by Jonathan Manske. ISBN-10: 0980194180

Happy for No Reason, by Marci Shimoff, ISBN: 1416547738

Ask and It Is Given, by Esther and Jerry Hicks, ISBN-10: 8190416944

Infinite Possibilities, The Art of Living Your Dreams, by Mike Dooley ISBN: 1582702268

The Compound Effect, by Darren Hardy ISBN-10: 159315724X

Discover the Power Within You, by Eric Butterworth, ISBN-10: 0061723797

The Field, By Lynn McTaggart. ISBN-10: 006143518X

You Were Born Rich, by Bob Proctor ISBN-10: 0965626415

The 4-Hour Workweek, by Timothy Ferriss, ISBN-10: 0091929113

The Happiness Advantage, by Shawn Achor, ISBN-10: 0307591549

Conversation with God, Book 1, by Neale Donald Walsch, ISBN-10: 0399142789

ctor, by Joe Vitale, ISBN: 0470286423

raction, by Michael J. Losier, ISBN-10:
    199737

The Power of Habit, by Charles Duhigg, ISBN-10:
    1400069289

Autobiography of a Yogi, by Paramahansa Yogananda ,
    ISBN-10: 0876120796

Manifesting 1,2,3, by Ken Elliott, ISBN-10:
    0989467007

Transform your Audience!

———

Author and professional speaker, James Anderson will show will show you how to create greater Happiness in your life by building new habits. You will learn about the Science of Happiness and how to raise your energy, passion, engagement in life and relationships, creativity and overall Happiness.

Invite me to come and speak to your organization or at your next event. Call me at 303-882-2885 or email me at jim@jamesranderson.net.

www.JamesRAnderson.net

www.ingramcontent.com/pod-product-compliance
Lightning Source LLC
LaVergne TN
LVHW091154080426
835509LV00006B/687